Getting back into "SF

H.M.S. Petard and the George Cross

by Peter Wescombe & John Gallehawk

CONTENTS

> *"This much is certain:*
> *He that commands the sea is at great liberty*
> *and may take as much and as*
> *little of the war as he will…………"*
>
> Francis Bacon, Lord Verulam 1561 – 1626

John Gallehawk B.Sc. was a statistician by profession.
Peter Wescombe B.A. is late of HM Diplomatic Wireless Service
Both are volunteers with the Bletchley Park Trust

> *"The dragon-green, the luminous, the dark,*
> *the serpent-haunted sea"*
>
> James Elroy Flecker 1884 – 1915

GETTING BACK INTO "SHARK", THE FOUR ROTOR ENIGMA

From August 1941, the British attack on the German three-rotor Enigma key "Heimisch" (Home), used by their Atlantic U-boats, and codenamed "Dolphin" by Bletchley Park, was successful in that decryptions greatly reduced Allied convoy sinkings in the Battle of the Atlantic. However, as early as the spring of 1941 Bletchley Park had been receiving indications that the Germans were considering introducing a four-rotor Enigma for U-boats operating in the North Atlantic and the Mediterranean, codenamed by them "Triton" and "Shark" by Bletchley Park.

During December 1941, a U-boat radio operator enciphered a message in "Triton", (it was not to be introduced until 1 February, 1942) realised his error and re-encyphered it in the current three rotor Enigma key.

Using these two fortuitous intercepts, Bletchley Park was able to work out the wiring of the fourth rotor.

However, the complexity introduced into codebreaking by the fourth rotor required a four-rotor Bombe to be designed and operating as quickly as possible if Bletchley Park was not to lose the initiative. Circumstances, i.e. insufficient three – rotor Bombes even to break current German Air Force/ Army and Naval Enigma keys, and the need to release experts from the urgent task of building them to tackle the four-rotor design problem, delayed this task.

Some success in breaking the "Shark" daily key had been achieved in Bletchley Park as early as December 1942, using a three-rotor Bombe, but it required twenty-six times longer to break a four-rotor key on this design of Bombe. American naval cryptanalysts were not fully trained on "Shark" until summer 1942, which left their vast resources in men and material untapped. It was June 1943 before the first four-rotor Bombe became operational in Bletchley Park, and August 1943 before one came on stream in Washington.

U-boats at sea were ordered to transmit weather reports. To shorten these messages they were encrypted in the three-letter group German Naval Meteorological Code before being re-encyphered in the current Enigma key. Thus a captured 1941 copy of the German Naval Meteorological Code became a valuable source of entry into Enigma traffic.

In 1942 the Germans introduced a new edition of the Met. Code, bringing the possibility of comparison with Enigma to a halt until the new code book could be recovered.

To compound the problem, the German equivalent of Bletchley Park, the Beobachtungs – Dienst (B-Dienst for short) successfully broke the Royal Navy's code No. 3.

This code was introduced in June 1941 as the common encryption system between British, Canadian and United States warships covering the Atlantic convoy routes.

The introduction on 1 February 1942 in the North Atlantic and Mediterranean, of the four-rotor Enigma, combined with the new 1942 German Meteorological Code and their breaking of the Royal Navy's Code No. 3, allowed the U-boat Command to plot the routes of our convoys, sometimes twelve hours in advance of their sailing, whilst we were now shut out of their intentions. It was the second great killing season for U-boat commanders in the North Atlantic.

If a four-rotor Enigma daily key-setting sheet could not be obtained, a copy of the new 1942 German Naval Meteorological Code was urgently required by the Allied cryptanalysts.

H.M.S. PETARD

H.M.S. PETARD & THE GEORGE CROSS

Setting the Scene

In the autumn of 1941, fifteen German submarines, some with Doenitz's most experienced crews, were sent to the Mediterranean. Among the more successful of these was U-559, a standard Type VIIC built by Blohm & Voss in February 1941.

Lieutenant Hans Heidtmann had been captain since commissioning. On his second cruise in the Atlantic, the U-559 sank the British freighter Alva but was attacked by three British destroyers and the crew rapidly learned what war was like as 180 depth charges exploded around them while they shivered 600 feet down. After twenty-four hours underwater they surfaced and returned to St Nazaire.

The U-559 then transferred to the Mediterranean and was based at the Greek port of Salamis. It was rumoured that in Salamis, donkey meat was used in salami issued to the sailors. For fun, they painted a white donkey on their conning tower.

At 4.00 p.m. on September 29th 1942, U-559 sailed from Messina on her tenth cruise and headed for the eastern Mediterranean south of Turkey, close to the Syrian port of Latakia. In spite of agent reports of potential targets Heidtmann did not sink any ships on this cruise. On October 29th, after asking him for a weather report, he was instructed to return to Messina after he had used up his fuel and armament. In the early hours of the thirtieth, U-559 surfaced and used its Short Weather Cipher to transmit the report.

A little before dawn, a Sunderland flying boat reported a radar contact "possibly a submarine" in the eastern Mediterranean roughly halfway between Port Said and Tel Aviv.

HMS Pakenham, with three other ships in company, including HMS Petard, were at sea at the time. Built in Newcastle and launched in March 1941, the Petard was one of eight P-class (for Pakenham) fleet destroyers. She had a handsome trawler bow, a single funnel and a top speed of 32 knots, with great manoeuvrability at high speed and stability in rough seas. Her main armament consisted of three, single 4-inch guns, but she was also well armed with eight torpedo tubes, one hundred depth charges and two sets of depth-charge throwers. Her crew consisted of nine officers and 211 ratings.

The captain, Lieutenant Commander Mark Thornton, was a Royal Navy career officer. He came to Petard having won a Distinguished Service Cross aboard another destroyer.

The first lieutenant was Antony Fasson, a Scot and an experienced career officer who exerted a firm discipline on his subordinates but also mixed easily with them, the junior officers found him a genial companion and Thornton considered him an exceptionally fine leader.

On the night of October 23rd, whilst en-route to Haifa, the four ships saw the sky erupt with artillery flashes at the start of the battle of El Alamein.

Following the Sunderland's enemy report of October 29th, they were diverted to the contact area.

SHIPS COMPANY H.M.S. PETARD, PORT SAID, EGYPT. OCTOBER 1942

The Hunt

It was a little after noon when the four destroyers reached the U-boat's reported position and began their sweep. Pakenham obtained the first asdic contact but Petard attacked first, at 12.57 p.m., dropping five depth-charges set to 250, 350 and 500 feet. After the explosions, the crew saw oil and heard a noise of escaping air – but saw no U-boat. A moment later, first HMS Dulverton, and then HMS Petard, dropped ten depth charges. The hunt went on for many hours while the air in the U-boat (bad at the best of times with the smell of unwashed bodies, old cigarette smoke, toilets, garbage, diesel oil, diesel fumes and cooking) grew even fouler.

Each attacking destroyer was directed by a cross-bearing of asdic contacts from two other ships. All hands topside scanned the sea for a periscope and torpedo tracks. When revolutions increased, men braced themselves against the shock of the underwater explosions.

As darkness fell, a member of the Petard's depth charge crew sent Thornton word that he thought the submarine was below 500 feet then the maximum setting on Royal Navy depth charges. He suggested that if he stuffed soap in the primers, the water pressure would build more slowly and the charges would sink deeper before exploding. He was granted permission to do so, and at 6.42 p.m. the Petard loosed ten "soaped-up" charges. The wait for the explosion was longer than usual but the trick worked, the U-Boat moved and contact was regained. Over the next four hours, four more attacks were made and the Petard ship's company felt the hunt was nearly up, time was running out for the U-boat.

In U-559, the crew counted 288 depth-charge explosions; the last ones holed the bow and stove in plates on the starboard quarter. The air was intolerable and it seemed as if the oxygen had run out. Heidtmann ordered the U-boat to surface.

The Petard's gun crew, the men on the bridge and the gun director team suddenly and simultaneously smelled diesel fuel: the asdic operators reported that they could hear a submarine blowing its tanks. Guns were trained on a port bow bearing. At 10.40 p.m. a patch of white water appeared, and in the darkness the port signal lantern picked out a conning tower, then the 36-inch search-light illuminated a U-boat with a white donkey painted on her conning tower. The U-boat's crew immediately abandoned ship. Thornton ordered his guns to open fire and the forward 4-inch hit the base of U-559's conning tower with their one shot but it rapidly became clear that she was being abandoned and further gunfire damage would make it harder to save her. Thornton ordered the boarding party away.

Petard's gun crew fusing 4" shells.

U559 being depth charged, October 1942.

The Bravery and the tragic Cost

First Lieutenant Fasson was on the starboard side aft, supervising the lowering of the whaler. The Captain ordered the gunnery control officer, Sub-lieutenant G Gordon Connell, to swim to the U-boat. As Connell started to strip, a young able-bodied seaman, Colin Grazier, joined him. Just then Fasson appeared and told Connell to take charge of the whaler and bring it around to the U-boat.

Within moments Fasson and Grazier had dived into the sea and were swimming across, with them was the sixteen-year-old NAAFI, canteen assistant, Tommy Brown, who had concealed his age to join the service. A few moments later the whaler, with German sailors clinging to it, reached the U-boat and made fast.

The U-boat was in desperate shape, with deck awash and rigging and wireless aerials completely shot away. The conning tower was a shambles; at the base was the 4-inch shell hole and there were two or three dozen inch-diameter punctures through which water sloshed. Plates on either side were stove in. In the darkness beyond, Petard's sister ships circled, listening for other U-boats.

Fasson and Grazier, now inside the U-boat used a machine gun to smash open cabinets in the captain's cabin and retrieve apparently secret documents from a drawer.
Tommy Brown carried these precious papers up the conning tower and gave them to the men in the whaler. Another sailor, K Lacroix, at the top of the conning tower, pulled up some books with a line. Brown made three trips to bring up more documents, managing to keep them dry despite the leaks and splashes. The water, which had been rising gradually, stood two feet deep on the inside deck. In the control room Fasson was trying to free an instrument from the bulkhead.

Brown told the lieutenant that those on U559's deck were telling them to come up, Fasson told him to take up the next batch of papers. The 'instrument' was hauled up on a line. By now the sea was over the afterdeck platform and Connell told Brown not to go down again but to tell Fasson and Grazier to get out at once.

Brown saw them at the bottom of the conning tower and twice shouted for them to come up.

They had just started up when, unexpectedly and swiftly the U-boat sank. Brown jumped off, Lacroix, still on the conning tower, had to pull against the water pouring down as he climbed the last two rungs of the ladder. He swam away against the suction, and he and Brown were picked up by the whaler.

Fasson and Grazier were unable to overcome the inrush of water. They went down with U-559.

They were posthumously awarded the George Cross. This is Britain's second highest decoration for bravery: because they had not acted in the face of the enemy they could not be awarded the Victoria Cross.

First Lieutenant Antony Fasson G.C.

Sub-lieutenant G. Gordon Connell.

U559's conning tower caught in Petard's searchlight, as she surfaced.

The Prize

The documents that had cost the lives of Fasson and Grazier included two which were to be extremly valuable to GC&CS. One was the current edition of the Short Signal Book. This was less useful immediately than the 1942 edition of the Short Weather Cipher that reached Bletchley Park on November 24th and led to cribs for the messages enciphered by the U-boats on the Four-rotor Enigma. From U559 documents Bletchley Park cryptanalysists learned that the four-letter indicators for regular U-boat messages were the same as the three-letter indicators for weather messages but with an added letter. Once a daily key was found for a weather message, the fourth rotor required testing in only twenty-six positions of the alphabet to find the full key. In BP it took until Sunday, Decmber 13th before tedious testing yielded the U-boat Engima key. Later that day, solutions to the four-rotor enigma U-boat key, code-named SHARK in BP, started to emerge. An hour later intercepts started to arrive at the Admiralty's Submarine Tracking Room revealing the position of fiteen U-boats. Over subsequent weeks, solutions again permitted evasive routing of our convoys and sinkings in January and February 1943 were halved from the high of the previous two months.

OMAS WILLIAM (TOMMY) BROWN, G.M.

E FAMILY

: Brown family, Thomas William his wife Margaret and their eleven children, lived
. flat in North Shields. Thomas William (Tommy), who was the eldest son, had
n born on the 4th December 1925 and was educated at the Western Board School.
left school at the age of fourteen years, and went to work in Leicester. Tommy's
ier was called up at the beginning of the war and posted to Persia (Iran) with the
/al Engineers.

MMY

941, still under sixteen years of age, Tommy volunteered for the NAAFI concealing
true age. In 1942 he was posted as a Canteen Assistant to HMS Petard, then serving
he Mediterranean. In October of that year his part in securing valuable cipher
terial from the U-559, brought to the surface by depth-charge attacks from HMS
ard and other British destroyers, earned a recommendation for the George Medal.
was two months short of his seventeenth birthday.

returned to the UK with HMS Petard in 1944 and was promoted to Senior Canteen
sistant before being posted to HMS Belfast which was then at Tynemouth
dergoing an extensive refit before sailing for the Far East in April, 1945. The
own's flat being close to the ship, Tommy was allowed to sleep at home each night,
urning to the ship the following morning. His father had recently been home on
ve and saw Tommy.

S TRAGIC DEATH

the early hours of Tuesday, 13th February 1945, Tommy, his mother and nine
thers and sisters were asleep in the North Shields flat when a fire broke out. All the
iily with the exception of Tommy and his four year old sister, Maureen, managed
:scape. Although she was eventually rescued by a neighbour, she was declared dead
arrival at hospital. Tommy died in the flames.

IE GEORGE MEDAL

hough it was Gazetted in September 1943, Tommy never did receive his George
:dal, Presumably, arrangements for the award ceremony were to have been made
n his return to the UK aboard HMS Petard in August 1944. The tragedy intervened
1 it was subsequently presented by King George VI to his mother in July 1945. In
35 his family presented the medal to the NAAFI Museum, together with his
npaign medals, where they remain to this day. His bravery was also recognised by
: NAAFI who presented the family with an engraved clock, which has since been
nated on loan to Bletchley Park, and is on display in 'B' Block.

TOMMY BROWN G.M.

ABOVE- HIS
CAMPAIGN MEDALS

FROM LEFT:
1. 1939-45 STAR

2. AFRICA STAR AND
   N. AFRICA CLASP

3. ITALY STAR

4. BURMA STAR &
   PACIFIC CLASP

5. 1939-45 MEDAL

BROTHERS STANLEY
AND DAVID BROWN
WITH DIRECTORS
AND THE
EX-CANTEEN MANAGER
OF HMS PETARD

LEFT TO RIGHT:
STANLEY BROWN
CAPT. MARTIN APPLETON RN
BRIAN WHITAKER-MD
TAFF CURTIS
DAVID BROWN

12